DISCUSSION GUIDE

Born Grown
The Making of Travis C. Burrell

Mentee/Student Edition

Discussion Guide Developed

by

Dr. Jo Evans Lynn, Ed.D.

ISBN: 978-1-7369837-3-7

Published by This1Matters Foundation, Greensboro, N.C.

INVATATION TO USE
Born Grown:
The Making of Travis C. Burrell
To Change Lives

Dear Reader:

This Discussion Guide allows you to share various aspects of your life in a way that respects your privacy and feelings. If read and shared as a guided reading activity, the book *Born Grown: The Making of Travis C. Burrell* has the potential to change the lives of youth everywhere.

Travis C. Burrell overcame enormous challenges to become a mentor, entrepreneur, and advocate for foster children and youth caught up in the criminal justice system. He is also a leader in his community. To reach his goals, he overcame some of the same issues that youth who spend their childhoods in neglectful homes and foster care must overcome.

The book should be an inspiration to every boy or girl in foster care and those who work with them, foster them, or teach them. Also, the book is a powerful tool in reinforcing our constant message:

"If you can dream it and are willing to work for it, you can achieve it."

Foster parents, undergraduate students in Sociology, child psychology, special education, regular classroom teachers, and mentors are being encouraged to read this book as part of their training or certification programs. If nothing else, the book will give those who serve children like Travis and his brothers a level of insight into their lives that will develop empathy.

Sincerely,

Dr. Jo Evans Lynn

PA BOOK REVIEW

Title of the Book: Born Grown: The Making of Travis C. Burrell

ISBN: ISBN: 978-0-578-66673-0

Formats: Softcover

Publisher: This1Matters Foundation

Language: English

Extremely Personal and Moving The uncomplicated writing and intimate storytelling will pull you into the book almost immediately. Born Grown is the biography of Travis C. Burrell that follows his journey from childhood through adulthood. The story unfolds with a 5-year-old Travis navigating the first day of school alone; he realizes that he does not come from a "typical" family. It continues to explore his life in foster homes and the complications and impact it had on him. The narrative is intensely personal and moving. It highlights how stifling and emotionally destructive neglectful homes are in a child's life. It occupies a child's mind and leaves a deep mark on his personality for the rest of his life. This book will make you feel deeply connected to the main character's struggles, adversities, and perseverance. It is heart-breaking yet hopeful and inspiring on another level. It uniquely enmeshes humor and sorrow. The authors will challenge your thoughts and views and make you understand how difficult and challenging life is for children in foster care; how it consumes all aspects of one's life. This book will resonate with you for a long, long time.

RECOMMENDATION: ★ ★ ★ ★ ★
Seal of Excellence: Yes
Level: Bronze

Contents

Calendar of Event 1

Synopsis 3

Discussion Calendar (With answers) 8

INTRODUCTION 5

ABOUT THE AUTHORS 5

Pre-Reading Discussion (Themes 7

Analytical Reading (Poetry) 12

Guided Listening Activity (Dear Mama) 14

Journal Writing 18

Discussion Questions 42

Narrative Writing 58

Summary/Enrichment Activity 60

Enrichment Discussion Questions 61

Born Grown Vocagulary Activities 62

Paideia Seminar 65

INDEX 68

Common Debate Rules for Classrooms 69

Narrative Graphic Organizers 71

Paideia Materials 72

Sample Posters 74

Calendar of Events

Kick Off! Travis C. Burrell, Motivational Speaker for all youth groups and Foster Parenting Groups or Dr. Jo Evans Lynn Motivational Speaker for Educators, Social Workers , Parental Groups and Undergraduate programs

Please Register online for Born Grown Events

Groups or organizations that want to plan an event with Travis Burrell or Dr. Jo Evans Lynn as speakers or facilitators, may schedule an event on the Born Grown website.

Please keep the following information in mind as you plan your event:

- Please check the online calendar to make sure that the date that you want for your event is available. Please remember to allow travel time between events. For example, if we are scheduled for an event in Dallas, Texas on Tuesday, it is unlikely that we would be available for an event in England on Thursday of the same week.
- **Travis C. Burrell , Motivational Speaker for all youth groups, Foster Parenting Groups, and Youth Advocate groups.**
- **Dr. Jo Evans Lynn Motivational Speaker for Educators, Social Workers, Parental Groups and Undergraduate programs**
- All events featuring either speaker must be scheduled at least 6 weeks in advance. Events featuring both speakers must be scheduled at least 3 months in advance)
- You will receive a confirmation/agreement form for your event within 48 hours after you schedule your event on-line. Please **sign and return a copy of the agreement within five business days.**

Sessions for reading and discussion of the book, Born Grown: The Making of Travis C. Burrell should be spread over a 3-6-week period. *We suggest that the groups are small with no more than 12 members and mentors or group leaders*

Aging out Essentials- Work & College Night (Fall & Spring), Transitional Housing, MEDICAID after Aging Out, Historically Black Colleges, Associate Degree Programs, post high school advance training programs (Police, firemen, etc.), and other work prep entities will be on hand to explain their incentives/programs to increase the numbers of underrepresented groups in their professions.

Lunch for Group (Foster Children, Social Workers, Foster Parents, etc.) (Picnic Lunch and Paideia Sessions with Box Lunches) at Local Park.

Essay Contest: One of the reasons why this book was chosen was because the lives of the main characters "mirror" the lives of many of the young people who live in foster care and in predominately black or brown Communities throughout America. Think about the main characters and the themes of the novel. Write a 1-2-page essay titled the "Empowering Foster Kids to Excel" discussing the role that social workers, foster parents, male mentors, coaches, relatives, and teachers have played in your life, the life of a relative or in the life of a close friend.

1

"We Are Family" Dinner, all participants and their foster families are invited for a weekend gathering. Each family will be asked to bring food that their family usually eats during their gatherings. For example, in the book Travis talks about the food produced by Byron's Mom, Grandma Woodlock and Mrs. Jackson , like succulent hot porkchops.

Men Work! Career Fair and College Night (Presentations at each Session). Careers like firemen, law enforcement, daycare, culinary arts , auto mechanics, etc. that need two years beyond high school or less will be featured along with Historically Black Colleges and Associate Degree programs.

Synopsis:

Born Grown is a biographical sketch that uses the memories and experiences of Travis C. Burrell to paint a very vivid picture of the lives of children who grow-up in neglectful homes and in-and-out of foster care. He had seen so much and been responsible for himself, his siblings, and a friend at such a young age that he felt that he was born grown. This life toughens the children who live them, desensitizes them, and matures them in ways that are difficult for others who have grown-up in other cultures to understand. The book is honest and real as told from the point of view of a five-thirteen-year-old. It will make you laugh and cry and hopefully do something to change the lives of children who are growing up like Travis.

Please read the pages noted below before each session so that you will be ready to engage in a scholarly discussion of the book.

Discussion Calendar

Sessions	Pages
Sessions	**Pages**
Session One	Introduction: Themes & Vocabulary
Session Two	Chapter 1- Essential Questions: Why aren't boys like Travis ready for school? What can parents and teachers do about it?
Session Three	Chapter 2- Essential Question: Do boys like Travis learn differently? Chapter 3- Essential Question: How long does early childhood neglect impact the education and lives of children?
Session Four	Chapter 4- Essential Question: How is the mother's attitude towards her children reflected in Travis' attitude towards his mother? Chapter 5- Essential Question: Are there factors in an individual's upbringing other than religion that prevents them from engaging in illegible behavior?
Session Five	Chapter 6- Essential Question: What factors cause a person to lose credibility? In other words, why aren't some people believed? Chapter 7- Essential Question: Why are the events in Chapter 7 particularly horrific?
Session Six	Chapter 8- Essential Question: To what degree do you believe the entire community shares responsibility for what happened to the boys in chapter 7? Chapter 9- Essential Question: What is a defense mechanism?
Session Seven	Chapter 10- Essential Question: Is it possible in advance to predict the success or failure of a foster care placement? Chapter 11: Essential Question: What are some strategies for building self-concept in young children?
Session Eight	Chapter 12- Essential Question: What are some reasons why a child should or should not be consulted about their placement?

Chapter 13- Essential Question: Can a person's attitude towards a situation affect the outcome?

Session Nine

Chapter 14- Essential Question: Why do people "see" what they want to see- missing evidence that is clear to others?

Chapter 15- Essential Question: In what ways are the changes in Travis and Anthony predictable?

Session Ten

Chapter16- Essential Question: What factors made the Jackson's an ideal placement for Travis and Anthony?

Chapter 17- Essential Question: What was the most important lesson Travis learned about life and family from staying with their Aunt Diane?

Session Eleven

Chapter 18: Essential Question: What factors made Sipes Orchard Home an ideal placement for the brothers?

Chapter 19: Essential Question: How would you explain Travis' choices in this Chapter?

Session Twelve

Chapter 20: Essential Question: Did this story end the way you expected it to end?

Paideia

Born Grown: The Making of Travis C. Burrell

INTRODUCTION

Travis and his brothers grew up in communities in Dallas, Texas , High Point, Hickory and Greensboro. North Carolina. His story teaches very vivid lessons about growing from boyhood to manhood in predominately Black communities during the eighties and nineties. However, the lessons of Black manhood– taking care of younger siblings, learning to survive, working to provide for one's family, and being emotionally connected to one's family are timeless.

This is a book about the power of family, community, foster care, education, and survival. This is a story about beating the odds and making a difference. It is a book about individuals changing their lives, and the lives of others ...together.

ABOUT THE AUTHORS OF BORN GROWN

Dr. Jo Evans Lynn, Jo Evans Lynn**, a native of Greensboro, N.C., taught nearly every grade level and every form of English/language arts during her 37 years in education. She graduated from James B. Dudley High School in 1967 and from Shaw University in 1970. She also received a master's degree in Reading Education from North Carolina A&T State University. She began her teaching career teaching middle school in Charlotte Courthouse, Virginia in 1972, but spent most of the early years of her teaching career in the Alamance County Schools teaching Title I Reading at Clover Garden Elementary School (9 years) and Reading Competency/College Prep English at Eastern Alamance High School (5 years). In 1987, she transferred and continued teaching Title I Reading, English, Journalism, Drama, and Speech & Debate at various high schools in the Greensboro City & Guilford County Schools in Greensboro, North Carolina (Grimsley Senior High School-10 years, James B. Dudley Senior High School-8 years, & GTCC Early/Middle College at Jamestown –2 years).

Her diverse experiences as a language arts teacher reinforced her belief that even fiction should be based on real life experiences. In all of her books, the reader shares her experiences during the 1950s & 1960s as an African-American child growing up on the "Colored" side of town in the segregated South and as a teen searching for a place in the world around her in which the rules of life and social order are changing almost daily. Although her subjects are sometimes both serious and controversial, her sense of humor and spiritual faith always shine through as she "speaks" to her readers about the realities of growing up poor and as the second eldest of seven children.

Travis C. Burrell considers himself to be a survivor of the foster care system and homelessness. Born in Dallas, Texas and raised in Highpoint, Hickory and Greensboro, North Carolina, he is now an advocate for both foster care and homeless youth. He considers himself to be a survivor of the foster care system and homelessness. He is now an advocate for both foster care and homeless youth.

At the age of 28, Travis began working with youth in the foster care system after realizing that many local youth were ending up homeless soon after aging out of foster care. In 2007, Travis founded *I Am Now, Inc.* a non-profit organization that provided services to homeless young adults, ages 16 through 23 in Guilford County, North Carolina. Soon after he started a transitional housing program for the young adult males, assisting them with successfully transitioning to independent living.

Travis has over 15 years of experience mentoring and advocating on behalf of youth, both locally and nationally. Serving as a public speaker, facilitator, and trainer for more than 10 years, Travis speaks on topics such as gang awareness, reversing personal power, foster care youth and homelessness amongst youth and young adults.

Pre-Reading Discussion

A theme is the central idea or ideas explored by a literary work. A work of literature may have more than one theme. Before we begin reading the book <u>Born Grown: The Making of Travis C. Burrell</u> by Jo Evans Lynn and Travis C. Burrell let us discuss some of the themes in relationship to your personal experiences, the experiences of friends or relatives or past reading.

Family is perhaps the most important theme of the book. The book examines family from all sides- the positive and the negative. Travis talks about his family, the people in his Hood, his relationships with his foster parents and his "neighborhood' whether it's the projects/public housing, an orphanage, a foster home setting or a group home. Based on your experiences with your family and neighborhood, which group do you predict will have the strongest impact on the behavior of Travis and his brothers in elementary school? In high school? After school?

Housing Projects: Housing that is built, operated, and owned by a government for low-income families and elderly occupants. Do you have Projects or low-income housing in your community? Do you know anyone who lives in public housing? Are children who live in public housing different from other children? Explain.

Reading Readiness: Reading readiness has been defined as the point at which a person is ready to learn to read and the time during which a person transitions from being a non-reader into a reader. Other terms for reading readiness include *early literacy* and *emergent reading*. Children begin to learn pre-reading skills at birth while they listen to the speech around them. In order to learn to read, a child must first have knowledge of the oral language. Examine the list of pre-school readiness skills. Were you or your children "ready" for preschool? If you cannot check-off 90% of the skills, explain why you feel you were or were not ready.

Language Skills

_____Speak in complete sentences and be understood by others most of the time

_____Use words to express needs and wants

_____Understand two-step **directions**

_____Make comparisons and describe relationships between objects like big/little, under/over, and first/last

Reading Readiness Skills

_____Enjoy listening to stories

_____Know how to find the first page of a book and which way to flip the pages

_____Recognize familiar logos and signs, like stop signs

_____Recite the alphabet and identify most of the letters

_____Recognize and try to write their own name

_____Recognize when two words rhyme (like *cat* and *bat*)

_____Start to **connect letter sounds to letters** (like the sound of the first letter in their name)

_____Draw a picture to help express an idea

Math Skills

_____Count from 1 to 10 without skipping numbers

_____Match a number to a group of five or fewer items ("I see three cats")

_____Recognize and name basic shapes (square, circle, triangle, rectangle)

_____Understand *more than* and *less than*

_____Arrange three objects in the right order (like from smallest to biggest)

_____Name or point to the colors in a box of eight crayons

Self-Care Skills

_____Use the bathroom and wash up on their own

_____Get dressed on their own (but may still need help with buttons, zippers, and shoelaces)

_____Know and can say their first and last name and age

Social and Emotional Skills

_____Separate from a parent or caregiver without getting overly upset

_____Interact with other kids

_____Pay attention for at least five minutes to a task an adult is leading, like listening to directions for an activity or discussing the day's weather during circle time

Fine Motor Skills

_____Use a pencil or crayon with some control

_____Use scissors

_____Copy basic shapes

_____Make distinct marks that look like letters and write some actual letters, especially the ones in their name

_____Put together a simple puzzle

Gross Motor Skills

_____Run

_____Jump with feet together

_____Hop on one foot

_____Climb stairs

_____Bounce a ball and try to catch it

Abandonment: Travis and his younger brothers are abandoned by both parents. Based on your personal experiences, reading, or the experiences of others, what effect might having been abandoned have on a child? On a family? Is it possible to have both parents living at home and still "feel" abandoned?

Drug Addiction: Drug addiction is a chronic disease characterized by compulsive, or uncontrollable, drug seeking and use despite harmful consequences and changes in the brain, which can be long-lasting. These changes in the brain can lead to the harmful behaviors seen in people who use drugs. Drug addiction is also a relapsing disease. Relapse is the return to drug use after an attempt to stop. Do you agree or disagree with this definition. Is drug addiction an illness or the result of bad choices?

Mentorship is another major theme of the book. A mentor is an adult who serves as a role model and advisor. Who has served as your mentor? Are your role models more likely to be celebrities or people in your immediate surroundings?

Poverty, especially the impact poverty has on living conditions, schools, crime, and opportunity, is an implied theme of the book. Is being poor the same as living in poverty? Explain.

Extended Family whether stable or unstable plays an important role in each of the lives of the authors. If you had to describe your family as a lifeboat, a Band-Aid, or wound which term would you use? Explain.

Choices and Consequences often people feel that everything is out of their hands- that they have no say so in what happens in their lives. However, *Born Grown: The Making of Travis C. Burrell* makes it clear that Travis and his parents made choices that made a difference in their lives. Think about some major choices that you have made thus far in your life. What were some consequences that you had to face as a result of your choices? Is the effect of your choices limited to your past or are you still affected by those choices?

Discipline, both self-discipline and parental discipline, is also a major theme. Which type of discipline do you think is most important for young people your age? Explain.

Foster Care is a temporary service provided by States for children who cannot live with their families. Children in **foster care** may live with relatives or with unrelated **foster** parents. Are you living or have you lived in foster care? If yes, describe your best or worst experience in foster care.

Survival Mechanisms a way of protecting oneself from being hurt by other people or circumstances. Travis and Anthony used forgetfulness or blanking out painful memories as a survival mechanism. What device or mechanism do you use to help you get through the worst of times?

The ability to dream big is another theme of the book. Some call it confidence; others refer to it as hope. Either way, it is manifested in one's ability to dream "big" beyond their present circumstances. What do you think happens to people who cannot dream beyond their current conditions? Why do people lose the ability to dream?

Perseverance is not only "hanging" in there through the bad times but fighting the good fight in the face of certain defeat. Often it is a matter of honor and ultimately one of the truest demonstrations of integrity.

Provider a parent who supplies sustenance (food, clothing, shelter, etc.) or support for their child or children. The breadwinner in a family.

Getting-by-One of the themes of the book has to do with "people doing what they have to do to get by." Is there ever a justification for breaking the law? Explain.

Cataloging is a poetic convention often used by rappers` listing similar items first used by American poet Walt Whitman.

Analytical Reading (Poetry)

Read the poem "A Dream Deferred" by Langston Hughes. The word *deferred* means, "to postpone or to put off until a later time." Answer the underlined question as it relates to your life or to the lives of people you know. What happens when we put our dreams off to a later time or when the dreams of those around us never seem to come true?

A Dream Deferred
by Langston Hughes

<u>What happens to a dream deferred?</u>
Does it dry up
like a raisin in
the sun? Or
fester like a
sore-- And
then run?
Does it stink like rotten meat?
Or crust and
sugar over--
like a syrupy
sweet? Maybe
it just sags like
a heavy load.
Or does it explode?

The questions are all *rhetorical questions* because they intend to answer the questions themselves.

Each question in the first stanza uses *simile*: "like a raisin in the sun," "like a sore," like rotten meat," "like a syrupy sweet." The second stanza which is not a question, but a suggestion also uses *simile* "like a heavy load." The last stanza uses *metaphor*, "does it explode?" The poem employs *rhyme*: sun-run, meat-sweet, load-explode.

The poem also uses *imagery*: "raisin in the sun," "fester like a sore— / And then run," "stink like rotten meat," etc.

By having Travis Burrell tell us about the various stages, events, and people in his life, the authors of the book, Born Grown: The Making of Travis C. Burrell use a unique method of helping the readers understand that although he had many things in common with the young people for whom the book was written, everyone has very special circumstances, attitudes, and perceptions of similar events that help "make" them.

Another major theme of the book is a boy's relationship with his mother and how that relationship impacts every aspect of his life. Listen as you read along with the lyrics of *Dear Mama* **by Tupac Amaru Shaku**

https://www.bing.com/videos/search?q=dear+mama&view=detail&mid=76112DBAC78DF9 38DC1576112DBAC78DF938DC15&FORM=VIRE0&PC=HCTS&cc=US&setlang=en- US&PC=HCTS&cvid=d245ab77ae624470950500b9e1e1a12b&qs=MB&nclid=120C6DA93 08D9096967CF32FD9F64467&ts=1587946414543

Discussion Questions Guided Listening Activity:

1. Why did the singer and his mother have a strained relationship during his youth?

_____

_____

_____

2. List at least three problems that young-single-mothers often experience.

_____

_____

_____

3. The song makes it clear that the singer's mother was a drug addict. Other than the fact that she was his mother, why do you think he still loved her and appreciated her?

_____

_____

_____

4. Tupac repeats the phrase "Though my shadow's gone, I'll never leave you." What do you think he means when he says, "my shadow is gone"?

_____

_____

_____

5. How do you think Tupac's relationship with his mother impacted his attitude towards women when he was a child and later in life? In what ways?

_____

_____

_____

Dear Mama

Tupac Shakur

When I was a youngin' me and my mama had beef

Seventeen years old kicked out on the streets

Though back at the time, I never thought I'd see her face

Ain't a woman alive that could take my mama's place

Suspended from school and scared to go home, I was a fool

With the big boys, breakin' all the rules

I shed tears with my baby sister

Over the years we was poorer than the other little kids

And even though we had different daddy's, the same drama

When things went wrong we'd blame mama

I reminisce on the stress I caused, it was hell

Huggin' on my mama from a jail cell and who'd think in elementary

Hey, I see the penitentiary, one day

And runnin' from the police, that's right

Mama catch me, put a whoopin' to my backside

And even as a crack fiend, mama

You always was a black queen, mama

I finally understand for a woman it ain't easy

Tryin' to raise a man you always was committed

A poor single mother on welfare, tell me how ya did it

There's no way I can pay you back

But the plan is to show you that I understand you are appreciated

Lady, don't cha know we love ya? Sweet lady

Dear mama, place no one above ya, sweet lady

You are appreciated, don't cha know we love ya?

Now ain't nobody tell us it was fair

No love from my daddy 'cause the coward wasn't there

15

He passed away and I didn't cry, cause my anger

Wouldn't let me feel for a stranger

They say I'm wrong and I'm heartless, but all along

I was lookin' for a father he was gone

I hung around with the Thugs, and even though they sold drugs

They showed a young brother love

I moved out and started really hangin'

I needed money of my own so I started slangin'

I ain't guilty 'cause, even though I sell rocks

It feels good puttin' money in your mailbox

I love payin' rent when the rent's due

I hope ya got the diamond necklace that I sent to you

'Cause when I was low you was there for me

And never left me alone because you cared for me

And I could see you comin' home after work late

You're in the kitchen tryin' to fix us a hot plate

Ya just workin' with the scraps you was given

And mama made miracles every thanksgivin'

But now the road got rough, you're alone

You're tryin' to raise two bad kids on your own

And there's no way I can pay you back

But my plan is to show you that I understand you are appreciated

Lady, don't cha know we love ya? Sweet lady

And dear mama place no one above ya, sweet lady

You are appreciated, don't cha know we love ya?

Pour out some liquor and I reminisce, 'cause through the drama

I can always depend on my mama

And when it seems that I'm hopeless

You say the words that can get me back in focus

When I was sick as a little kid

To keep me happy there's no limit to the things you did

And all my childhood memories

Are full of all the sweet things you did for me

And even though I act crazy

I gotta thank the Lord that you made me

There are no words that can express how I feel

You never kept a secret, always stayed real

And I appreciate, how you raised me

And all the extra love that you gave me

I wish I could take the pain away

If you can make it through the night there's a brighter day

Everything will be alright if ya hold on

It's a struggle everyday, gotta roll on

And there's no way I can pay you back

But my plan is to show you that I understand you are appreciated

Journal Writing

Note to Readers:

Talk to your friends, siblings, or teammates about an event or period in your life that you shared that not only had an impact on who you are now but may also impact your future. For example, some young men might write about how each of them came to be involved in the group that is reading this book or about how the events in Middle School or their freshman year in high school helped to mold them into the individual they are today.

Activity Directions: *Keep a journal of **at least six entries** about people (friends, family, teachers, mentors) and events that have had an impact on your life. Other than deciding what you will write about as a group, do not read one another's journals until each of you has written about the same topic.*

Suggested Topics:

1. Are you an older or younger sibling in your family? Are the duties, expectations, and responsibilities different for you than for your siblings?

2. We are friends because… (Write about you relationship with your best friend. When and how did you become friends. How do you help one another? What are your strengths or weaknesses as friends?

3. Starting with the most important, make a list of the top ten things every parent should do.

4. This one time… (Write about a time that you got into BIG trouble with a sibling or a friend. What were the consequences? What did you learn from this experience?)

5. We will always be friends because…. (What will hold you and your best friend together as friends after high school?)

6. This is my "big" dream" and here is how I will make it happen…

7. I grew up the day that… Write a 1-2-page epiphany story detailing the single event that, for you, marked your transition from childhood to adulthood. (An epiphany story)

8. This is my definition of a "real" father…

9. My_____(Title: Teacher, Coach, Father, Uncle, Neighborhood, Pastor, etc.) was a "Real Father to me because…

10. The importance of father figures is an underlying theme of the book. Is having father figures more important for boys than for girls? Explain.

11. From your personal experience, or from the experiences of friends or family members describe the components of a "good" foster home. What should the foster parent(s) be like? How should they treat foster children? Should there be limits on the number of foster kids in a home? Include anything that you feel is important.

Please supply 1-2 additional topics that you want to write about. (Optional)

_____

_____

_____

_____

_____

_____

_____

_____

Journal 1

Journal 2

Journal 3:

_____

_____

_____

_____

_____

_____

_____

_____

_____

_____

_____

_____

_____

_____

_____

_____

Journal 4

Journal 5

Journal 6:

_____

_____

_____

_____

_____

_____

_____

_____

_____

_____

_____

_____

_____

_____

Journal 7:

Journal 8:

_____

_____

_____

_____

_____

_____

_____

_____

_____

_____

_____

_____

_____

_____

Journal 9:

Journal 10:

_____

_____

_____

_____

_____

_____

_____

_____

_____

_____

_____

_____

_____

_____

Journal 11:

_____

_____

_____

_____

_____

_____

_____

_____

_____

_____

_____

_____

_____

_____

DISCUSSION QUESTIONS

Pre-reading
Note: In most cases the answers will vary for parts or all of a question.

1. What does the term "The Hood" mean to Travis and his brothers? Does the term *the hood* mean the same to you and your friends?

2. Who are the men in your life that are teaching you how to treat the women in your life?

3. Using the **prereading discussion,** define the term *Hood* in your own words.

4. According to the synopsis, why did the author feel that he was Born Grown? In other words, what does he hope his audience will gain from reading the book?

Chapter 1

1. What does the fact that Travis arrived at school alone and in unwashed clothes tell us about his home life?

2. Travis defines friendship *as one friend taking care or protecting the other friend.* Think about your relationship with your best friend. Why did the two of you become friends? Define friendship based on your relationships with your best friend and your other friends.

3. Why did the teacher decide to call Travis Mister Travis? Think about your elementary school teachers. What do you think they would have done under similar circumstances?

4. At the beginning of the school year, the teacher referred to Travis as a *blank slate*. At the age of five, are children truly blank slates? Explain.

5. In the first chapter of the book, we begin to see evidence of what is important to Travis. Briefly discuss what we know about his values at this juncture of the book.

Chapter 2

1. Why are small celebrations of successes important to young children?

2. Although Travis seemed like an old soul, in what ways was he like other children his age?

3. Why do you think Travis decided to give a special thank-you to Mrs. Echols after the other students and parents were gone?

4. Why didn't Travis want the Mrs. Echols to take him home?

5. This chapter begins to establish the impact that Travis' mother had on Travis' viewpoint of motherhood and women.

https://www.youtube.com/watch?v=XW--IGAfeas

Many consider this song to be one of the deepest rap songs ever made and it is often referenced by other artists in their work, building Shakur's persona as a very socially conscious and influential rapper. The song was voted #11 in About.com's Top 100 Rap Songs, with "Dear Mama" was voted #4.

As you listen to the song again, try to catalog (list)...

Cataloging the reasons why women deserve respect:

1. _____

2. _____

3. _____

4. _____

5. _____

6. _____

7. _____

8. _____

Cataloging ways women are disrespected:

1. _____

2. _____

3. _____

4. _____

5. _____

6. _____

7. _____

Keep Your Head Up by Tupac

Little somethin' for my godson
Elijah and a little girl named Corinne

Some say the blacker the berry, the sweeter the juice
I say the darker the flesh then the deeper the roots
I give a holler to my sisters on welfare
Tupac cares, and don't nobody else care

And uhh, I know they like to beat ya down a lot
When you come around the block brothas clown a lot
But please don't cry, dry your eyes, never let up
Forgive but don't forget, girl keep your head up

And when he tells you you ain't nuttin' don't believe him
And if he can't learn to love you, you should leave him
'Cause sista you don't need him
And I ain't tryin' to gas ya up, I just call 'em how I see 'em

You know it makes me unhappy
(What's that?)
When brothas make babies and leave a young mother to be a pappy
And since we all came from a woman
Got our name from a woman and our game from a woman

I wonder why we take from our women
Why we rape our women, do we hate our women?
I think it's time to kill for our women
Time to heal our women, be real to our women

And if we don't we'll have a race of babies
That will hate the ladies, that make the babies
And since a man can't make one

He has no right to tell a woman when and where to create one
So will the real men get up
I know you're fed up ladies but keep your head up

Keep ya head up, ooo, child things are gonna get easier
Ooo, child things are gonna get brighter
Ooo, child things are gonna get brighter

Aiyyo, I remember Marvin Gaye, used to sing ta me

He had me feelin' like black was tha thing to be
And suddenly tha ghetto didn't seem so tough
And though we had it rough, we always had enough

I huffed and puffed about my curfew and broke the rules
Ran with the local crew and had a smoke or two
And I realize momma really paid the price
She nearly gave her life, to raise me right

And all I had ta give her was my pipe dream
Of how I'd rock the mic and make it to tha bright screen
I'm tryin' to make a dollar out of fifteen cents
It's hard to be legit and still pay tha rent

And in the end it seems I'm headin' for tha pen
I try and find my friends but they're blowin' in the wind
Last night my buddy lost his whole family
It's gonna take the man in me to conquer this insanity
It seems tha rain'll never let up
I try to keep my head up and still keep from gettin' wet up

You know it's funny when it rains it pours
They got money for wars but can't feed the poor
Say there ain't no hope for the youth
And the truth is it ain't no hope for tha future

And then they wonder why we crazy
I blame my mother, for turning my brother into a crack baby
We ain't meant to survive, 'cause it's a setup
And even though you're fed up
Huh, ya got to keep your head up

11. What does Tupac say will happen to boys who grow up hating and disrespecting the ladies?

45

Chapter 3

1. How do we know that his father's abandonment was particularly traumatic for Travis?

2. Why do you think Travis took the time to describe his father? What do you feel is most significant about his father's looks?

3. How long did it take for the boys to become really worried about their father's failure to return? Why did it take so long?

4. How did their mother's behavior change?

5. A sympathetic character is one for whom the reader feels empathy or that the reader cares what happens to him or her? At this point in the book, which character do you feel is the most sympathetic?

6. After reading pages 17-19, do you consider Travis' mother a sympathetic character? Explain your reasoning.

7. Why were the Turners never robbed? Can you think of anyone in your neighborhood who is loved by everyone? Tell us a little bit about what makes or made him or her special.

Chapter 4

1. Travis did what he could to make sure that his brothers had food. Why didn't he make sure that his mother got something to eat?

2. Why didn't the people in Turner Housing report the parent's neglect? What do you think the people in your neighborhood would have done in similar circumstances?

3. Why wouldn't Travis take more food from Byron's Mom? What does this tell the reader about his character?

4. List the two events that changed Travis' ability to care for his brothers.

5. Writers often include what is called "comic relief" before or during traumatic events. What is comedic about Miss Towns' narrative about Mrs. Turner's death?

6. How did Hambone and Inkie define the term "indefinitely"? What does each man's definition tell the reader about their personalities?

Chapter 5

1. What was an easy method Travis could have tried to get food for himself and his brothers? Why didn't he choose to use this method.

2. Why did the Church Lady give Travis food in spite of the fact that she knew he was lying about getting it for his grandmother?

3. Why do you think Travis' mother tore-up the food stamps? Do you think your mother would have done the same thing? Explain.

4. Travis and Anthony took turns going to school. How do you think this arrangement impacted the education of both boys?

5. Why was Travis certain that he would "ace" the test? Why didn't he do as well as he could have done?

6. On a scale of 1-10 with 1being unprofessional and ten being professional rate the school phycologist's attitude and behavior while testing Travis. Explain your rating.

7. At this point, Travis' educational philosophy is "I learned everything I ever will need to know in kindergarten. Now school is a waste of my time." If you had an opportunity to talk to a young man who felt this way about education, what would you say to him?

8. What evidence is there that the boy's situation was becoming more and more desperate?

Chapter 6

1. How do the two older boys respond to their mother's return?

2. Although Byron's Mom is introduced in the first chapter, the reader does not learn her name until Chapter 6. Why do you think a formal introduction is needed at this point in the book?

3. Why did Travis open the door for Maylene Trivett in spite of the fact that his mother told him not to open it?

4. Since the neighbors had mostly left Lisa Burrell and her children alone, why had someone called Byron's Mom?

5. Why did Travis and Miss Maylene doubt his mother's version of how she was injured?

6. One theme of the book is the impact of a young man's relationship with his mother on his opinions and treatment of women later in life. Briefly discuss Travis' attitude toward his mother at this point in the book.

7. The sense of smell can bring back pleasant memories. Recall a particular smell that brings back a cherished memory and discuss that smell and memory with your group.

8. Why did Travis have a panic attack on the way to the shelter?

9. What didn't Travis like about the shelter? What did he like about it?

10. Why do you think their mother left the shelter after a few days?

Chapter 7

1. When Travis' mother returned at the beginning of Chapter 7, why was Travis hopeful that things would get better?

2. What does Travis' description of the man who came home with his mother suggest about the man?

3. Why was the man willing to take Rodney and not Travis and Anthony?

4. What advice did their mother give Anthony and Travis? Why didn't they immediately follow her advice?

5. At what point did Travis suspect that something was wrong? Why do you think it took him so long?

6. What aspects of their childhood, do you think, enabled Travis and Anthony to survive the events at the end of chapter 7?

Chapter 8

1. Why do Ham Bone and Inkie hesitate to enter the alley? What makes up their minds?

2. Why do they decide not to report the assault to the police?

3. Is this fear of the police common in your neighborhood? In your opinion, is the fear justified? Explain.

4. Talk to an older woman (70's and up) about Miss Mae Ella or the woman in their neighborhood when they were growing up who served the same role. Is there a Miss Mae Ella in your neighborhood? Why or why not.

5. How did Miss Mae Ella deal with the problem? Would you have handled it differently? Explain.

Chapter 9

1. How did Travis and Anthony decide to deal with what had happened to them?

2. Why do you think Mr. Herman made a joke of the way the boys looked?

3. How did Miss Rivers explain her role to the boys? Why didn't they believe her?

4. What did she do to gain their confidence?

5. What made the Buckner Home for Children seem like another world to Travis?

Chapter 10

1. Why wasn't the first foster home a good match for Travis and Anthony?

2. Why didn't the foster home with Mrs. Keel work out? If you had to place blame for this failure on someone, on whom would you place the blame?

3. Why was it so difficult for the boys to have faith in God or conceptualize "going to hell."

4. The women in Travis' life set his life-long standard for beauty. Compare and contrast his descriptions of two of the women (Mrs. Echols, His Mother, Ma Turner, Miss Woodlock).

5. What evidence is there that Travis' placement in Special Education was inappropriate?

6. Explain what you believe are the two most important factors in their successful placement with Miss Woodlock.

Chapter 11

1. What did Miss Woodlock do to help build the boy's self-concept?

2. Read the Foster Parent's Pledge on pages 88-89. Give each of Travis and Anthony's foster parents a grade A-F. Explain your grades.

3. What was Travis' favorite part of the vacation that they took with Miss Woodlock? Why do you think it was his favorite part?

4. At first, Travis and Anthony weren't happy about Miss Woodlock becoming their Mom. Why?

5. How does Miss Woodlock manage to get Travis and Anthony to behave?

Chapter 12

1. Why didn't Travis "let" Anthony win sometimes?

2. Why didn't Travis believe Anthony when he said that a police officer was making Miss Woodlock cry?

3. Who was the policeman? What reason did he give Miss Woodlock for taking the boys?

4. What did Travis think was his real reason for removing them from Miss Woodlock's care?

5. What did the boys take with them to High Point? Do you think this will be an important factor later in the book?

6. Since Travis did not cry, how do we know that he was very upset about being removed from Miss Woodlock?

Chapter 13

1. Why was Travis upset about moving into another housing project?

2. What experiences, according to Travis, do all people in drug infested neighborhoods share?

3. Have you ever been placed in a situation that you "just knew" was bad for you? Explain.

4. It only took his mother two weeks to get back to using drugs. How did she hide her usage from her brother?

5. Why didn't Travis believe that his uncle was fooled? Do you agree or disagree with him?

Chapter 14

1. Why was Travis so angry? Do you feel that his anger was justified?

2. What seemed strange about the woman who came to take the boys away from Juanita Hills?

3. Why did the boys go with the stranger?

4. What details about their Aunt Ruth make her a sympathetic character?

5. What convinced Travis that there was a God somewhere?

6. When Travis said, "It was the gun that did her in" what did you expect to happen?

7. Did the final event in this chapter change your opinion of their Uncle John? Explain.

Chapter 15

1. Compare and Contrast Mrs. Jackson and Miss Woodlock.

2. How do we know that Mrs. Jackson has a sense of humor?

3. Why did Travis and Anthony call Mrs. Jackson The Church Lady?

4. Why did Travis and Anthony consider Mr. Jackson their "first model of manhood'?

5. Why didn't Anthony like sports?

Chapter 16

1. What factors in the second time that Travis was tested for Special Education led to a different outcome?

2. Why was Anthony taken out of special education classes too?

3. How did their placement in regular classes change the boys' attitudes about school and their ability to learn?

4. Since he could afford them, why didn't Mr. Jackson get the boys Air Jordan tennis shoes. What lesson do you think he wanted them to learn?

5. Why did the boys' bedroom smell ten times worse than the city dump? What did Mrs. Jackson do to ensure that it never happened again?

6. How did both boys change while they were with the Jacksons?

7. Why did Mrs. Jackson start bank accounts for both boys?

Chapter 17

1. For the second time, an adoption is stopped so that the boys can be placed with relatives. Divide the group into teams: Pro (For) or Negative (Against) and debate the following resolution:
    Resolve that: The general welfare of children is best served by placing them with relatives.
    Research to back up your opinion with facts and think about how you will respond (rebuttal) statements that contradict your position.

2. What changes did their Aunt Diane make to accommodate the three boys. How were the other families supposed to help her?

3. What was the most important thing Travis learned from being with his Aunt Diane?

4. Why wasn't she able to keep the boys?

Chapter 18

1. Why did the boys end up all the way in Hickory, North Carolina?

2. Describe Sipes Orchard Home.

3. The three years that they are in Sipes is the longest time since they were 6, 5, and 1 that they have lived together. In what ways does Travis change during this time?

4. In what ways does he remain the same?

5. Why does Travis work three jobs? What does he do with his money?

Write a two-three paragraph essay discussing the impact of teammates, friends, coaches, and mentors in a young man's life using supporting details from the book.

_____

_____

_____

_____

_____

_____

_____

_____

_____

_____

_____

_____

_____

_____

_____

_____

_____

_____

_____

_____

_____

_____

_____

_____

_____

_____

Chapter 19

1. How did Chaz get Travis to run away with him?

2. Why did Travis end up living on the street?

3. What made Play Low different from Chaz and his cousins?

4. Why wasn't Travis afraid that summer?

5. How did he find his niche for his business?

6. What factors made him successful?

7. Can you think of other professions that he could use these same skills to earn a living?

Chapter 20

1. What two events changed his perspective of dealing drugs?

2. Why do you think Travis went with Chuck?

3. How does Travis feel about his future at the end of the book?

Narrative Writing Activity

The excerpt about Mrs. Towns telling people her version of what had happened to Ma Turner inserts a degree of humor that is called "comic relief." Dr. Lynn often uses humor to soften the impact of some of the most horrific events in her writing. As a pre-writing activity use the Graphic Organizer for this Narrative Writing Activity located in Index (Stories Straight From My Hood).

1. In two-three paragraphs relate a story from your youth that makes you smile or laugh years later even though at the time it happened it did not seem funny. Share your story with the group.

_____

_____

_____

_____

_____

_____

_____

_____

_____

_____

_____

_____

_____

_____

_____

_____

_____

Summary Enrichment Activity

1. In one or two paragraphs, briefly explain the lessons found in the book and how they could or could not be applied to your life. Discuss what you have written in your journal and talked about with your group. Did anyone talk about getting something different out of the selections in the book than you did?

_____

_____

_____

_____

_____

_____

_____

_____

_____

_____

_____

_____

_____

_____

_____

_____

_____

_____

Enrichment Discussion Questions

1. Peer pressure plays an enormous role in the lives of young people in every circumstance. How did it play into Travis' life?

2. Education, both formal and informal, is at the center of this success story. Teachers like Miss Echols, and some of his other teachers nurtured and inspired. However, less prevalent teachers were those who "...just didn't know how to reach boys like him and didn't seem to care. Travis explains, "They expected and accepted that we were slow learners and could learn very little, we usually gave no more." Why do you think Travis felt this way? To what degree are teachers—and students—to blame for this situation? Does the book suggest any ways to improve the system?

3. After reading this book, what do you conclude is required to enable other young people in rough environments to achieve? Who is ultimately responsible for providing those opportunities? The individual? The family? The society? The government ?

Born Grown: The Making of Travis C. Burrell

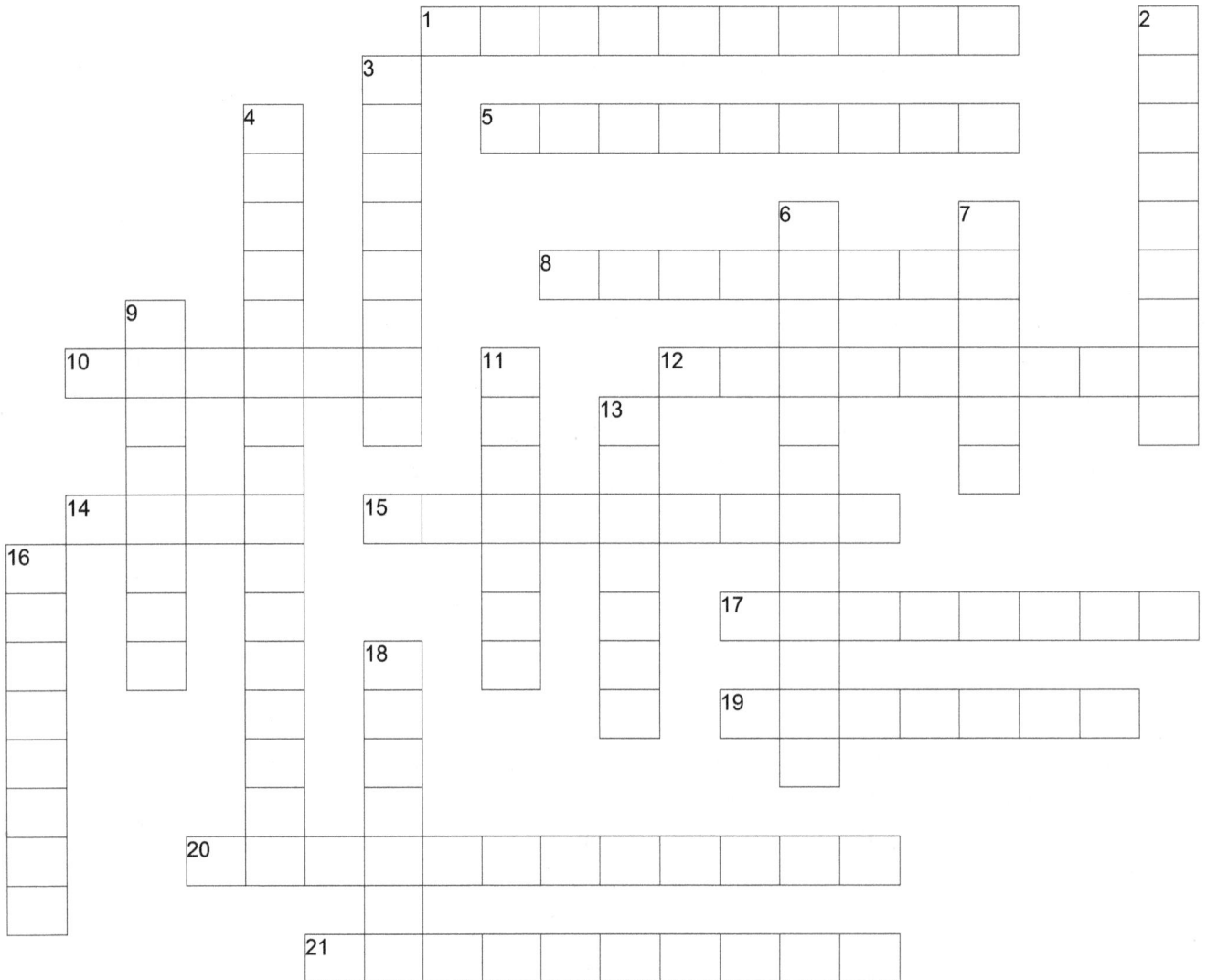

Across
1. To get done or achieve
5. Guardian or defender
8. Possible or reasonable
10. An expert or really capable person
12. Habit, compulsion, obsession
14. Slang for where you live
15. A residential home for children
17. Detained by the police
19. A government assistance program
20. For the foreseeable future or for ever
21. A nick name used to hide ones identity

Down
2. People who stand-in for parents
3. Tear up or damage
4. Program for remedial education
6. Early or entry level formal education
7. Counselor, supporter, guide
9. Thinking clearly
11. Admiration; to have a high opinion
13. Handouts, aid from an agency
16. Housing for low income families & the elderly
18. Lack of care

WORD BANK

Hood   Projects   Mutilate   Addiction   Neglect   Mentor

Special Education   Savant   Kindergarten   Protector

Charity   indefinitely   feasible   Respect   guardians

orphanage   arrested   accomplish   Street Name   Welfare

Rational

Born Grown: The Making of Travis C. Burrell

```
n m s t h o o d d t c e l g e n w
o f a c c s r s t c e j o r p c i
i s v e d t w o c h a r i t y y e
t e a p e r w n t m y t w s k l a
a n n s t e s o g n f u v k l e b
c e t e s e o i l t e v f k b t j
u t a r e t r t m n l m g r l i f
d r i e r n p c b r m t m l e n g
e a f e r a h i m i k s a l r i u
l g f t a m a d r n d n b c a f a
a r u a f e n d t p o i y k f e r
i e t l i e a a p i s i a k l d d
c d s i a l g o t a r d u u e n i
e n f t h s e a e t p m w d w i a
p i y u d f r f i b a s n n d k n
s k j m s n p r o t e c t o r v s
r b c b r a c c o m p l i s h d s
```

Rational   Welfare   Street Name   accomplish   arrested   orphanage
guardians   Respect   feasible   indefinitely   Charity   Protector
Kindergarten   Savant   Special Education   Mentor   Neglect   Addiction
Mutilate   Projects   Hood

Paideia Seminar: Born Grown
Suggested Post Reading Activities

Pre-activities
- The mentees will review the goals for Seminar.
- The mentees will review the Paideia Seminar rubric (see Index).
- Mentees will set a personal goal for the Seminar.
- Mentor will state the objectives for reading the book
  Mentee will read the book, *Born Grown: The Making of Travis C. Burrell*

Activities
Seminar
1. Once the students have read the book , the mentor shall pose an opening question to begin the Seminar: "Of the themes that we discussed in the Pre-Reading Activity, which one do you think the authors would agree was the single most important lesson for readers to learn? What leads you to believe that?"

2. Once the discussion gets going, the mentor can ask more questions to guide the discussion in the proper direction. These questions will also check the students' comprehension of the text.

> How did family relationships influence Travis' life? What stands out to you about his childhood experiences at home and in foster care?

> Throughout the book Travis describes a turning point at which specific decisions or choices—to be responsible for his brothers, to refuse to respond to his test, to leave Sipe's Home, to sell drugs—changed the course of his life. Are such moments recognizable only in hindsight? Do you think that shaping the events of your life into a story would influence the importance you placed on specific events?

3. Before the discussion ends, the mentor should ask the following closing questions:
- What are the consequences for allowing "family expectations" or peer pressure to influence your decisions?
- How does it affect the lives of the characters in the book?
- How have "family expectations" or friends who are being brought up differently from you affected your life?

Research project
1. The mentees will select a person who has changed the lives of others. They will conduct on-line research and write an essay which will discuss what the individual had to overcome to be successful and how this person has impacted the lives of others. The essay should focus on one or more of the

themes of the book, *Born Grown: The Making of Travis C. Burrell* {Family, abandonment, foster care, drug addiction, education, service to others, role models, consequences, etc.) and link to the theme of their own lives.

2.   Students will use the information in their essay to produce a presentation that incorporates technology and writing skills, in order to inform the group about the individual they researched.

Assessment

Mentor will evaluate individual performance during Seminar by using the Paideia Seminar rubric (see list of materials/resources)

Mentees will complete a self-evaluation by using the Personal Seminar Rating Chart (see list of materials/resources)

INDEX

COMMON DEBATE RULES FOR CLASSROOMS 69

NARRATIVE GRAPHIC ORGANIZER 71

Paideia Materials 72

Hooping to Succeed Tournament Poster 74

COMMON DEBATE RULES FOR CLASSROOMS

Common Courtesy During Debate

Debates often focus on controversial topics that students may feel passionately about, so courtesy and respect for all opinions should be encouraged. To introduce the idea of courtesy, explain to students that debate questions often do not have a "right" or "wrong" answer and that critical thinking develops when different ideas are present. For example, set ground rules for interrupting, raised voices and personal attacks before starting the debate. The High School Public Debate Program allows heckling limited to a single word or phrase directed at the judges. However, interruptions or exclamations that disrupt the speaker or are excessively rude are not allowed. The penalty for breaking rules in competitive debate include taking a loss, having to repeat the debate or a reprimand.

2 Rules for Topics

Rules for choosing topics attempt to ensure that both the pro and con sides of the subject can be researched. In classroom debates, teachers provide the topics, often based on the class subject. For example, in an English class, students may debate whether fate actually guides the human experience after reading *Oedipus Rex.* In a history class, students may debate the merits of war, while a science class may debate the ethics of bioengineering. When choosing topics for the classroom, teachers should take into account the political climate of the school as well as the maturity and sensitivity of the students involved. Teachers should also avoid topics that reveal personal bias or may easily lead to attacks on individual students.

3 Argument and Proof

With an assigned topic, both the pro and con sides in the debate should begin to research evidence for their side of the argument. Debaters should use both facts and opinions in the presentation of their argument. Students should also research the opposing side and perform a critical analysis to decide which facts and opinions of the other side will be used in the rebuttal stage. In competitive debate, the use of electronics during debate is not allowed, but classroom debates may allow this. Evidence should be in the form of facts, not other speeches, or opinions, and the first mention of evidence should include a complete citation -- author, title, date of publication and page number.

4Rules for Speakers

To ensure that all opinions are heard, develop a format for engaging in debate and introduce the format to the students before the debate. For example, the debate may include two rounds of discussion in which the first side presents the "pro" side immediately followed by the team with the "con" side. The second round will allow the "pro" side to respond to the "con" arguments of the first round. Create time limits for each side that are clear and carefully adhered to. For example, give each side a two-minute limit to present its case.

STORIES STRAIGHT FROM MY HOOD!

Characters
Who or what will be in my story?

Setting
Where will my story happen?

Problem
What will happen to my characters?

Solution
How will my characters handle the problem?

Paideia Seminar Rubric

CONDUCT

Students sits in seminar style.

Student looks at person talking and listens to learn.

Students waits for turn to speak. Student is polite.

1   2   3   4   5

LISTENING

Students looks at person who is speaking.

Students asks questions about what has been said.

Student talks about what he or she has heard.

1   2   3   4   5

SPEAKING

Student speaks clearly with appropriate voice level.

Student expresses complete thoughts.

Students comments relate to the text, questions, or previous statements.
Student's comments show respect for self and others.

Student asks questions.

1   2   3   4   5

CRITICAL THINKING

The student's response reflects listening to the text and beyond the text.

The student's response reflects listening to others.

Student can explain why he or she disagrees with another student and can support it from the text.

Student response reflects comprehension of text; answers are thought out.
Student makes statements that indicate application to real world situations.

1   2   3   4   5

1 = not yet   2 = occasionally   3 = often   4 = frequently   5 = always

Personal
Seminar Rating Chart

Personal Goals:

Rate yourself 1 - 5, with 1 being your BEST and 5 being your WORST. Be honest !

_____ I came prepared for seminar.

_____ I was courteous to the other group members.

_____ I paused and thought before speaking.

_____ I listened to others tell their ideas.

_____ I kept an open mind for opinions different from my own.

_____ I acted as a positive role model for other students.

_____ I built on other ideas before I gave my own opinion.

_____ I reflected on the text.

_____ I felt comfortable speaking during seminar.

_____ I spoke clearly.

_____ I interrupted others.

_____ I acted silly.

_____ I did not look at the person speaking.

_____ I spoke off topic.

_____ I talked too much.

Did I meet my personal goal?

Hooping to Succeed

When: Saturday, September 4, 2021
7:30a.m.-12:30p.m.

Where: Barber Park, 1500 Dan's Road, Greensboro, NC 27401

What: College Tour Fundraiser

Mid -Elite 7th-8th Grade
Elite 9th-12th Grade
Grand Elite (Two or More Varsity Level Players)
Super Elite (Two or More College Players)

Why: There are a few career prep courses at all high schools.
These programs include many gifted students for whom
a professional career may have been an impossible dream.
However, there are not enough spaces in these classes for all of the
students who want to take the courses to enroll.

Our goal is to raise enough money to help support additional career

*prep courses and a College Tour to ensure that any student who is willing to do
the hard work and studying that it takes to have a profession when they
graduate from high school or continue on to college has financial support to
make his or her dream*

www.ingramcontent.com/pod-product-compliance
Lightning Source LLC
Chambersburg PA
CBHW081650270326
41933CB00018B/3417